Marriage Scriptures

"What God has joined together,
let no man put asunder."
— *Matthew 19:6*

Marriage Scriptures

"What God has joined together,
let no man put asunder."
— Matthew 19:6

BETTY-ANN BERAZZAH

MARRIAGE SCRIPTURES
"What God has joined together, let no man separate."
Matt. 19:6

Betty-Ann Berazzah
93-35 219 Street
New York, NY 11428

Unless otherwise indicated, all scriptural quotations are from the New King James Version of the Bible.

iUniverse books may be ordered through booksellers or by contacting:

iUniverse
1663 Liberty Drive
Bloomington, IN 47403
www.iuniverse.com
844-349-9409

Cover design by:
James Emilien
Cover illustration is protected by the 1976 United States Copyright Act.

Book production by:
Silver Lining Creative
www.silverliningcreative.com

ISBN: 978-1-4401-1399-4 (sc)
ISBN: 978-1-4401-1401-4 (hc)
ISBN: 978-1-4401-1400-7 (e)

Print information available on the last page.

iUniverse rev. date: 06/15/2022

DEDICATION

I dedicate this book to my Heavenly Father.

I pray that every person reading this book will receive the blessings that He desires to bestow upon them, through this book.

I pray that His anointing will flow through every word that is written for His people.

I pray that loving hearts between husbands and wives will be restored, and they will have a new season of restoration for their marriages.

CONTENTS

Dedication

Acknowledgments

Introduction 1

Gratitude 7

Colossians 1:9,10, Hebrews 10:26-29 8

Genesis 2:24,25 12

Matthew 19:3-9 14

Matthew 14:3-11 18

Matthew 5:31,32, Mark 10:2-12 20

1 Corinthians 7:39,40 24

Romans 7:2-3 26

Hosea 3:1-3 28

Hosea 14:1,2 30

Hosea 14:4-7 32

Luke 16:18 34

Romans 12:9-11 36

1 Corinthians 7:10-14.............................38

Ephesians 5:22-33 41

Colossians 3:8,12,13-15,18,19...............42

1 Thessalonians 4:3-8 44

Titus 2:4,5 46

Hebrews 13:4 48

1 Peter 2:11,12 50

1 Peter3:1..52

1 Peter3:4..54

1 Peter3:7..56

1 Peter 3:8,9,12,13 58

Deuteronomy 24:1-4 62

"God Hates Divorce" — Malachi 2:14-16 64

"Friendship" — Songs of Solomon 5:16.......66

Proverbs 2:10-13..................................68

"The Harlot" — Proverbs 5:3-6 70

"Your Own Wife" — Proverbs 5:15-20........71

"The Harlot" Proverbs 6:24-29 72

"The Crafty Harlot" — Proverbs 7:10-27......74

"Adultery" — Proverbs 30:20 76

"A Virtuous Woman" — Proverbs 31:10-31 78

Revelation 2:21-23 80

Isaiah 54:4-8 83

Isaiah 54:10-15 84

Ecclesiastic 2:26 86

Ephesians 4:26, 29-32 89

"Love" — 1 Corinthians 13:4-8 93

Conclusion 97

This is My Prayer 101

Acknowledgements

First and foremost, I give thanks to God.
All Glory and Honor to my Heavenly father for the wisdom and knowledge
He has blessed me with, to do and complete this assignment.

Thank you to my Spiritual Parents,
Pastor John H. Boyd, Sr. and Mother Marjorie Boyd,
of New Greater Bethel Ministries,
For your prayers and guidance.
For the impartations of Love for God's people and the Love of Souls,
For teaching us how to live Righteous and Holy,
For being a good shepherd over us, your flock.

Jeremiah 3:15 —"I will give you Shepherds according to my heart, who will feed you with knowledge and understanding."

I thank God for blessing me with a shepherd after His own heart.
Thank you Elder John Boyd, Jr. for your words of encouragement and strength.
You all have touched my life, and I know you will continue to touch
many more lives as you did mine.
May God Bless You All.

Marriage Scriptures

"What God has joined together,
let no man separate."
— Matthew 19:6

INTRODUCTION

This book was inspired by God for *His* people. It is written for *His* children who have a desire to please Him; for those whose souls are hungry for *His* knowledge and power; to the saints who want to live by *His* Word; for *His* people who desire for themselves, the same life that God desires for them. God's Word, the Bible, is His desire for us, His children. We are His children.

EPHESIANS 1:13 — *"In Him you also trusted, after you heard the word of truth, the gospel of salvation."*

This book is not intended for just anyone; it is intended for the people who desire the blessing and fullness of God in their life. It is not for the people who want to give partial obedience to His Word. Some people pay their tithes, go to church regularly, serve in the church, read the Word of God regularly, but with regards to the *"sanctity of marriage,"* they are not fully aware of what God desires for their marriage, or what role God assigned them to, in the *"church of marriage."* (I said "church of marriage" because God values marriage next to the church.) Nature's instinct tells us, in marriage, "Do what everyone else is doing; treat their wives and husbands as the rest of the world treats theirs." No one is to blame, because the Bible states we will perish for lack of knowledge.

HOSEA 4:6 — *"My people are destroyed for lack of knowledge."*

Most people are not aware of the sacredness of marriage, how God views marriage, or how God wants us to live daily with our wives and husbands. How bad do you want God, what are you are willing to sacrifice to have a relationship with Jesus Christ? Are we willing to live by the true Word of God, or are we willing to do what the rest of the world is doing? Do we care about living our lives on this Earth to please God or to please the world? Are we living a life where half of our body is trying to please God and the other half, the world?

Our flesh has become a problem in our lives; our flesh produces nothing good. Do we desire to do the "Will of God" for our lives? *The "Will" is the desire to do good.* Do we have the ability to do good? We all have the ability to do good and to do what God wants us to do, but sometimes we lack the desire, and fall short. It is God's desire for us to do **His Will** and live by **His Word of truth**.

I attended a meeting at my church one evening. We were asked if anyone had a testimony that they would like to share, and a gentleman got up and shared his testimony about his divorce from his wife. He said that his ex-wife is not cooperating with him in their divorce matter; she did not want to sign the divorce documents. His testimony was 'his ex-wife finally signed the documents.' Then, he said "I had to divorce her because the Holy Spirit told me to divorce her."

When he said this, immediately the Holy Spirit began speaking to me. The Holy Sprit said to me, "This is not of Me." Tell my people what my Word says about marriage. I want you to put together My scriptures for marriage." The Holy Spirit began bringing to my remembrance, scripture after scripture. God honors marriage; it is His command that you leave your father and mother and cleave to your wife of your youth, and if God joined you to your wife of your youth, the Holy Spirit will not tell you to divorce your wife of your youth, since God hates divorce.

MALACHI 2:16 — *"For the Lord God of Israel says, that He hates divorce."*

If you choose to divorce, it is a choice *you* made. It is a fleshly choice. God hates divorce, but He loves divorced people. God loves us all unconditionally. It blesses God when we desire to do His will and live by His Word.

I couldn't wait to get home; scriptures and words began flowing into my heart. After the service, I had to write all that was flowing into my heart. I kept hearing these words over and over, *"tell my people, tell my people."* This book was born out of all that the Lord said to me that night and the days to follow.

I believe in my heart that God has already pre-assigned each person that He wants to have this book, before it was ever written or printed. If God gave the vision for this book, it means He already has the recipients for the blessings. I am just a humble and willing vessel.

Mother Theresa said these words, and I quote, "We are like pencils in God's hands; He uses us to write in the World."

To God be the glory for this book. I am just a vessel.

I come to you my brothers and sisters in love, not condemnation; because God loves us.

HEBREWS 12:6 — *"For whom the Lord loves, He chastens."*

No one is to be condemned, since we all have made mistakes, we all have sinned and fall short of His Glory.

ROMANS 3:23 — *"for all have sinned and fall short of the glory of God, being justified freely by His grace through the redemption that is in Christ Jesus."*

All that God wants is for us to acknowledge our sins, repent, turn away from the sins that we have repented for, and acknowledge His truth, the Word. Search His word, know what He desires of us, and do it.

JOHN 4:23 — *"Worship the father in spirit and truth.*

I have put together some scriptures that would enlighten you to better understand and enter into a blessed marriage; build a stronger marriage on a foundation in Christ; and restore broken marriages.

"THE WORD WILL WORK FOR YOU IF YOU WORK THE WORD."

When you are finished reading this book and you feel a touch from God to draw unto Him by turning away from any sin in your life, or any misconceptions that you might have about marriage, consider it to be the *"Love of God"* for you, that He is chastening your heart through conviction by the Holy Sprit, to be obedient, to do what is right, and live righteous and holy.

Imagine this; God created us. He gave us His written Word in the Bible, and some of us choose not to read His Word. He is still finding other ways to reach us with His words through preaching, teaching and books. Isn't He a God that loves us dearly, to chase after us with such passion because He wants us to have knowledge of Him.

God does not gain anything from us; He does not need anything from us. We need God; we have everything to gain from God. God does not need everlasting life, He is everlasting life; we want everlasting life; we want to spend eternity in heaven with God the Father and Jesus Christ, the Son.

We should be the ones chasing after God and desiring to be obedient to *His* word and staying in *His* will, so we can inherit our blessings and have eternal life. If someone told you that they had a large inheritance for you, do you think that person would be chasing after you to give you an inheritance? Shouldn't you be the one seeking to find the person and enter into a relationship with that person, so that you can receive your inheritance? Look at the big picture here. God has so many blessings in store for us. We should seek to find Him and build a relationship with Him.

To the youths who are thinking about beginning a new life in marriage, this is a good place to begin by knowing what values should be placed in marriage and the strong commitment that comes with marriage. It is not a vow that you can make today and re-consider tomorrow as society leads the youths of today into thinking. It is a life-long *Covenant, Commitment*, and *Choice*. It is a choice because there is no command that you must marry; it is a choice. But it is a choice that comes with *sacrifice, consequences and rewards*. The choice is yours to make, and yours to keep, till death do you part. We need to humble ourselves before God and serve Him with an attitude of gratitude for our lives and everything in it, including our *Marriage*.

Marriage was designed to be a triangle, God to the top, husband and wife coming under the Godhead.

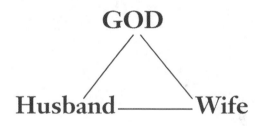

"GRATITUDE"

Gratitude unlocks the fullness of Life

It turns what we have into enough, and more.

It turns Denial into Acceptance,

Chaos into Order,

Confusion to Clarity,

It can turn a Meal into a Feast,

A House into a Home,

A Stranger into a Friend.

Gratitude makes sense of our Past,

Brings Peace for Today,

And Creates a Vision for Tomorrow.

COLOSSIANS 1:9,10

"For this reason we also, since the day we heard it, do not cease to pray for you, and to ask that you may be filled with the knowledge of His will in all wisdom and spiritual understanding;

that you may walk worthy of the Lord, fully pleasing Him, being fruitful in every good work and increasing in the knowledge of God."

HEBREWS 10:26-29

"For if we sin willfully, after we have received the knowledge of the truth, there no longer remains a sacrifice for sins,

but a certain fearful expectation of judgment, and fiery indignation which will devour the adversaries.

Anyone who has rejected Moses' law dies without mercy on the testimony of two or three witnesses.

Of how much worse punishment do you suppose, will he be thought worthy who has trampled the Son of God underfoot, counted the blood of the covenant by which he was sanctified a common thing, and insulted the Spirit of grace?"

To any one who sins deliberately after receiving the knowledge of the truth is to totally reject or depart from God. Those who choose to disobey God's knowledge of truth have become his adversary and will face the judgment of fiery anger from God. How much punishment would someone receive who treats the Word of Christ with disrespect or disdain?

MARRIAGE SCRIPTURES

*M*arriage is the capstone of the family, the building block of human civilization. A society that does not honor and protect marriage undermines its very existence. Why? Because one of God's desires for marriage is to show the next generation how a husband and a wife demonstrate reciprocal, sacrificial Love towards each other.

(A "capstone" is a stone that forms the top of a wall or building; a finishing stone of a structure; a crowning achievement, point, or element.)

When we hear the word "Marriage" we think of celebrations, flowers, dresses, suits, food, cakes, and limousines. We have a fantasy of a husband coming home with his pay check and giving it to the wife to pay all the bills, the husband brings home roses on a Friday afternoon, and everyone lives happily ever after. But marriage is more than this. After the ceremony and celebration, we come to the "real deal." ***The part that requires unconditional love, respect, compromise, patience, sacrifice, union, commitment, communication, staying married till death.*** *The only way out of marriage should be through death, not divorce.* Marriage is a covenant that we should enter into with great seriousness and earnest prayer.

If you are unmarried, and you plan to get married some day, or you are seeking God for a husband or wife, I plead with you, "Pray about it first."

PROVERBS 3:6 —"In all your ways acknowledge Him, and He shall direct your paths."

Ask God to send the person that He has chosen to be your husband or wife. Ask God to cancel all plans and tricks that the enemy might have, to send a counterfeit husband or wife. Every blessing that God has for us, Satan has an "imitation" of it. We have to be aware of the devices of the enemy, and be able to discern God's blessing as opposed to "the imitation."

When we pray, the enemy is always lurking around to know whatever information he can about us. And if he finds out you are seeking a mate, "Be aware."

1 PETER 5:8 — "because the adversary the devil walks about like a roaring lion, seeking whom he may devour. Resist him."

If you ask God for a husband or wife, and you see your prayer being anwered, begin to acknowledge God. Be sure he/she is from God. Ask God if he or she is the person He has chosen for you, pray about the person before you make any future plans. Be sure that you get an answer from God before you decide to begin wedding plans. Let God direct your path and your footsteps before entering a marriage. This is a serious commitment and covenant to God.

Many times we become infatuated by the person we become attracted to, and we decide to enter into marriages that are not of God, then problems arise, and we want to get out of the marriage. But, if we acknowledge God in the beginning of any relationship and let Him guide us to choose the husband or wife that He has chosen for you, God will take us through the marriage, even when the stormy days come. When a marriage is ordained by God, He puts a seal on your marriage and there is no room for separation or divorce. God will stand true to His Word; He will make sure everything that is broken, will be repaired and everything missing will be restored. Guaranteed! God will finish what He has started. God will take you through a marriage that is ordained by Him, "till death do you part."

PHILIPPIANS 1:6 — "being confident of this very thing, that He who has begun a good work in you will complete it until the day of Jesus Christ."

Marriage is a fusion of two histories: the unification of two cultures and backgrounds; but most of all, it is the union of two destinies.

When two destinies come together, and we put God and His Word, the Bible, in the mix, can you imagine the great impact the two destinies could have on the world.

Live for God; Let God's Word direct your Marriage; and you can be an impact to nations.... It takes two, to agree. "Can two walk together, unless they are agreed?" Amos 3:3

God wants to give the sanctuary of marriage back to His people. He wants to give back the years in marriages that the enemy has stolen. See, the enemy knows if he destroys marriages, he separates what God has joined together. He can only separate us from God through sin, anger, bitterness, rejection. God wants to give back the love between husbands and wives. For all the husbands and wives who missed their season of a blessed marriage, God wants to give you a new season, a second chance. Even if divorce found its way into your marriage, God still loves you, no matter what, and He still desires to bless you. We are still his children. We were all fearfully and wonderfully made by God. If every individual person would invite Jesus Christ to live in their hearts, then the power of God through the Holy Spirit would work in them. This is the foundation we need to stand firm on when the storms and trials of marriage come. The big question is *"What is God's ideal for marriage? What does God expect from us in marriage? What does the Bible say about marriage?"*

GENESIS 2:24,25

"Therefore a man shall leave his father and mother and be joined to his wife and they shall become one flesh."

And they were both naked, the man and his wife, and were not ashamed.

*T*hese words were spoken by God to Adam and Eve in the Garden of Eden in the beginning of time. This is where the foundation of marriage began. This is where the bond of marriage of two becoming one flesh began. It is God's desire for marriage. It was God's desire for the union, love and for the marriage to be sacred.

Everything on this earth began with a spoken word from the mouth of God. This is where God first introduced "marriage" to Adam and Eve; this was the first example of marriage. Marital bonding becomes imminent, and man and woman now becomes "we", no longer 'me and you."

The duty of wives is submission to their husbands in the Lord, which includes honoring him, from a principle of love to God and to the husband. The duty of husbands is to love their wives. The love of Christ to the Church is an example, which is sincere, pure, and constant.

MATTHEW 19:3-9

The Pharisees also came to Him (Jesus), testing Him, and saying to Him, "Is it lawful for a man to divorce his wife for just any reason?"

And He answered and said to them, "Have you not read that He who made them at the beginning 'made them male and female,'

and said, 'For this reason a man shall leave his father and mother and be joined to his wife, and the two shall become one flesh'?

So then, they are no longer two but one flesh. Therefore what God has joined together, let not man separate."

They said to Him, "Why then did Moses command to give a certificate of divorce, and to put her away?"

He said to them, "Moses, because of the hardness of your hearts, permitted you to divorce your wives, but from the beginning it was not so.

And I say to you, whoever divorces his wife, except for sexual immorality, and marries another, commits adultery; and whoever marries her who is divorced commits adultery."

*A*dam and Eve was the first example of marriage created by God and any other example is wrong. What God has created for us in marriage and everything on this earth is best for our souls and should be followed accordingly, because it was ordained by God this way, to prepare us for, and preserve us for the Kingdom of heaven. The teachings of the gospel by Jesus Christ, if we really embrace it, makes us want to bear burdens, and bear the infirmities of those whom we are connected to in marriage; to consider their peace, joy and happiness more that our own. Marriage is a covenant that we should enter into with great seriousness and earnest prayer.

Three reasons why married people should remain married:

1. God made *male and female (Genesis 5:2)*. If God had intended for Adam to have many wives, He would have made more women and allow him to choose how many wives he wanted. The same goes for Eve. God created man and woman; God created marriage: Creator means He is The Lord, and the one who determines what is the ideal for *marriage*.

2. God ordained marriage as the strongest bond in all human relationships. He said "A man should leave his parents and be *joined to his wife*. *"Leave"* means "to abandon," *"join to;"* means "to be glued to." The language is very clear and strong here. The most permanent relationship in this world is not between parent and child, but *between husband and wife*.

3. The two shall become *"one flesh."* The basic element here in marriage is a contract or covenant.

Jesus points out in this scripture that Moses never commanded divorce; he permitted it because of the hardness of man's heart. God's original ideal was that married couples would *not* divorce. God loves a broken and a contrite heart, not a hard heart. God sometimes allows what is less than *His* ideal, because people's hard heart made God's ideals unattainable. Jesus shows us here that Moses' law allowed divorce, but it was not meant to use this as permission; it was only used in the state of hardness of heart.

PSALMS 51:17 — "The sacrifices of God are a broken spirit, a broken and a contrite heart, these O God you will not despise."

If you have hardened your heart towards your husband or wife, it means you are not aligning yourself with what God loves and requires of you.

The statement *"Except for sexual immorality"* pertains to Jesus' statement of a reason to acquire a divorce, not a reason for remarriage as many people may think. The "exception" refers directly to the choice to obtain a divorce, if there is sexual immorality in a marriage. The exception does *not* say because there was sexual immorality, you are allowed to remarry. *The words sexual immorality is attached to grounds for divorce, not grounds for remarriage.*

1 CORINTHIANS 7:10 — "Now to the married I command, yet not I but the Lord: a wife is not to depart from her husband. But even if she does depart, let her remain unmarried or reconciled to her husband. And a husband is not to divorce his wife.

Many people think that the "exception" automatically makes room for remarriage. The world has taken the gospel and made it convenient to their needs and often the Body of Christ follows the world out of convenience. Take the time to find out what God's Word, the Bible, truly is saying and desiring for us to do. The statement of "exception" validates the grounds for divorce that is being questioned by the Pharisees; where Moses *permitted* divorce, not commanded. The ultimate issue should not be the right to divorce, but God's original desire for husbands and wives to be one flesh. "One flesh" is the language of family ties and alliances (2 Samuel 5:1).

The Genesis principle from which Jesus draws this application not only opposes divorce; it opposes marital disharmony altogether. *Matthew 10:34-39 and 19:27-30*, shows that one's relationship with a spouse must take priority over any other relationship except one's relationship with Christ. Jesus' opponent assumes that whatever the law addresses, it permits. Jesus responds that Moses permitted this merely as a result of Israel's hard heart. God's ideal was always that we should avoid divorce; the preservation of a marriage depends on both parties wills. Jesus' point here is to underline in no uncertain terms, the sanctity of marriage and our solemn responsibility to preserve it at all cost.

When we hold grudges against a genuinely repentant spouse (which is, the one that God joined you with from your youth) and remain hardhearted toward her or him, whether or not we officially cast the person away, we hinder our own communication with God. It is no coincidence that in the book of Matthew, Jesus' teachings on marital commitment directly follows his teaching on forgiveness *Matthew 18:21-35.*

This scripture tells exactly what God's ideals for marriage and divorce is, and it is an extended confirmation of what Jesus spoke in the Matthew 19:9. This is clearly stated in the following verses of *1 Corinthians 7:10-14.*

1 CORINTHIANS 7:10-14 — Now to the married I command, yet not I but the Lord: A wife is not to depart from her husband.

But even if she does depart, let her remain unmarried or be reconciled to her husband. And a husband is not to divorce his wife.

But to the rest I, not the Lord says: If any brother has a wife who does not believe, and she is willing to live with him, let him not divorce her.

And a woman who has a husband, who does not believe, if he is willing to live with her, let her not divorce him.

For the unbelieving husband is sanctified by the wife, and the unbelieving wife is sanctified by the husband, otherwise your children will be unclean, but now they are holy.

COLOSSIANS 3:13 — "bearing with one another and forgiving one another."

EPHESIANS 4:32 — "And be kind to one another, tenderhearted, forgiving one another, even as God in Christ forgave us."

The bond which God has tied is not to be untied. Let those who are putting away their wives and husbands, consider what would become of themselves, if God should deal with them in the like manner.

MATTHEW 14:3-11

"For Herod had laid hold of John and bound him, and put him in prison for the sake of Herodias, his Brother Philip's wife.

Because John had said to him, "It is not lawful for you to have her."

And although he wanted to put him to death, he feared the multitude, because they counted him as a prophet.

But when Herod's birthday was celebrated, the daughter of Herodias danced before them and pleased Herod.

Therefore he promised with an oath to give whatever she might ask.

So she, having been prompted by her mother, said, "Give me John the Baptist's head here on a platter."

And the king was sorry; nevertheless, because of the oaths and because of those who sat with him, he commanded it to be given to her.

And his head was brought on a platter and given to the girl, and she brought it to her mother.

*J*ohn the Baptist was beheaded because he told Herod the King, "It is not lawful to have his half brother's wife." Herod went to Rome where he met Herodias, the wife of his half brother Philip. After seducing Herodias, Herod divorced his own wife and married her. John had rebuked the king for his moral transgressions and so John the Baptist was beheaded and his head presented on a platter upon request by Herodias' daughter prompted by her mother Herodias.

Be aware that we will be persecuted for compromising the truth; the truth being God's word. John the Baptist was persecuted because he told the Godly truth about sexual immorality and took a stance for what God's word says. It was a high price to pay. But, Jesus paid a high price for us, because he loved us.

MATTHEW 5:31,32

"Furthermore it has been said, 'Whoever divorces his wife, let him give her a certificate of divorce.'

But I say to you that whoever divorces his wife for any reason except sexual immorality causes her to commit adultery; and whoever marries a woman who is divorced commits adultery."

MARK 10:2-12

The Pharisees came and asked Him, "Is it lawful for a man to divorce his wife?" testing Him.

And he answered and said to them, what did Moses command you?"

They said, "Moses permitted a man to write a certificate of divorce, and to dismiss her."

And Jesus answered and said to them, "Because of the hardness of your heart he wrote you this precept.

But from the beginning of the creation, God 'made them male and female.'

'For this reason a man shall leave his father and mother and be joined to his wife,

and the two shall become one flesh;' so then they are no longer two, but one flesh. Therefore what God has joined together, let no man separate."

In the house His disciples also asked Him again about the same matter.

So He said to them, "Whoever divorces his wife and marries another, commits adultery against her.

And if a woman divorces her husband and marries another, she commits adultery."

*J*esus indicates that God's original purpose for marriage was that the union should not be broken. But, if by the hardness of your hearts, you give a certificate of divorce, Jesus clearly states that you are not to remarry and if you do, man or woman, you will be committing adultery and whoever you marry will also be committing adultery.

He did say if you divorce your wife for any reason except sexual immorality, you will cause her to commit adultery if she remarries another man or remains unmarried and indulges in sinful sexual immorality. If a man or woman divorces a husband or wife because of sexual immorality, he or she would not be causing him or her to commit adultery because he or she has already committed adultery, prior to the divorce. But it is not God's ideal for man to commit adultery, and so, this is why He does not like divorce, because divorce leaves the two parties open to the world to indulge in sexual immorality, which is not of God.

Once a man or woman is divorced from husband or wife, this leaves room for the enemy to step in, in the form of harlots with their lips dripping with honey, *(Proverbs 5:3)* seducing you into sexual sin. After a certificate of divorce is given, both husband and wife are open to the world of sin. Any sexual relation that you enter into after divorce from the husband or wife that God first joined you to, is adultery. Once there is sexual interaction taking place with someone other than the person you *leave your mother and father and cleave to* — the wife or husband of your youth God joined you to — in God's eye, it is adultery.

When God said, "leave your mother and father and cleave to your wife," He is telling us that the only time you leave your mother and father's house is in your youth. This is about the time where you are beginning to develop into adulthood, so this means that the only marriage God honors is your first marriage, because this is the marriage that occurs right after you leave your mother and father. And this is the husband or wife you should cleave to, explained in *Malachi 2:14 "Because the Lord has been witness between you and the wife of your youth," "Proverbs 5:18 "and rejoice with the wife of your youth."* This is the marriage that God honors; this is the marriage which God glues you together with, for life. This is the marriage you made a covenant to God in. Has God ever broken any of His covenants to us? How could we break our covenant to Him? Then He goes on to say *"therefore what God joins together, let no man separate."* This simply means — and there is no simpler way to explain it, study it yourself, meditate on it — it simply means that the marriage that God honored first, after you leave your mother and father, the person that God joined you to, glued you to, the marriage that you first made a covenant to God in, is the marriage that is sacred in God's eye, sanctified and blessed by God. Any marriage after the one God blessed — you are on your own.

MARK 10:9 — *"Therefore what God has joined together, let no man separate."*

Let us take a closer look at this verse. It is as if God is giving us a command and a warning in one. He is telling us what He has joined together, do not attempt to separate it or bring division to it, (here he is speaking directly about marriage). The unspoken message in this verse says if you disobey His command by attempting to separate or bring division to anything He has joined together (marriage), there will be a price to pay because He is a sovereign God, and all disobedience to His commands and words comes with a price to pay. My friends, do not allow yourselves to be the one to cause division, or separation between a husband and a wife. If you are a mother-in-law, father-in-law, sister-in-law, friend, woman or man, do not allow satan to use you to cause separation in a marriage. There will be a great great price to pay from God.

REVELATION 2:22,23 — *"Indeed I will cast her into a sickbed, and those who commit adultery with her into great tribulation, unless they repent of their deeds.*

I will kill her children with death, and all the churches shall know that I am He who searches the minds and hearts. And I will give to each one of you according to your works."

Divorce is a choice by man that was permitted by Moses because of the hardness of their hearts. Divorce is permitted, but God looks at what you do after divorce. Look at what Jesus said to the Pharisees, *"Whoever divorces his wife and marries another, commits adultery against her. And if a woman divorces her husband and marries another, she commits adultery."*

The only place in the Bible that remarriage is spoken of, is where a marriage partner dies, that is, *only* if you become a widow or widower.

ROMANS 7:2,3 — *"For the woman who has a husband is bound by the law to her husband as long as he lives. But if the husband dies, she is released from the law of her husband.*

So then if, while her husband lives, she marries another man, she will be called an adulteress; but if her husband dies, she is free from that law, so that she is no adulteress though she has married another man."

"Therefore what God has joined together, let no man separate." This means that when God puts His hands to something and blesses it, a certificate of divorce given by a court of law cannot separate a marriage. The court of law is made by man; man, woman or harlot cannot separate what God has joined together. The husband or wife who wants to please God can choose to forgive his or her husband or wife.

The book in the Bible that highlights God allowing remarriage is in the book of Ruth, where Ruth married Boaz after her husband died.

Let no one think or make excuses for getting into adulterous situations. Stand up and be responsible for entering into temptation of lust, and sexual immorality, divorcing your husband or wife to marry someone else. Any sexual immorality that you get into is a choice that you made.

JAMES 1:14,15 — *"But each one is tempted when he is drawn away by his own desires and enticed.*

Then, when desire has conceived, it gives birth to sin; and sin, when it is full-grown, brings forth death."

COLOSSIANS 3:14 — *"Bearing with one another, and forgiving one another if anyone has a complaint against another; even as Christ forgave you, so you also must do. But above all these things put on love, which is the bond of perfection. And let the peace of God rule in your hearts to which also you were called in one body; and be thankful."*

PHILIPPIANS 3:13 — *"Forgetting those things which are behind and reaching forward to those things which are ahead, I press towards the goal of the prize of the high calling of God in Christ Jesus."*

1 CORINTHIANS 7:39,40

"A wife is bound by law as long as her husband lives; but if her husband dies, she is at liberty to be married to whom she wishes, only in the Lord.

*T*his scripture from the Bible tells us a wife is bound to her husband while he is alive. The only time that she is not bound by the law of her husband is when he dies. While he is alive, even if she chooses to separate from her husband she is still bound by her husband until he dies.

When he dies, that is the only time a wife is scripturally at liberty to remarry. This is a very important scripture that everyone in the 21st century should know. *This is a very important scripture.* The world would not agree with this scripture, because the world has created its own laws, but, what does God's word say? God is speaking to you in this scripture.

ROMANS 7:2-3

"For the woman who has a husband is bound by the law to her husband as long as he lives. But if the husband dies, she is released from the law of her husband.

So then if, while her husband lives, she marries another man, she will be called an adulteress; but if her husband dies, she is free from that law, so that she is no adulteress, though she has married another man."

This is God, the Heavenly Father speaking. It is understandable what He wants to say. These are not man's words, these are the words spoken by God. God is trying to let us know in these last days what He requires of us. After receiving this knowledge, we will be charged with this word, because now we know the truth. The Word of God is the Truth. We will be held accountable for the knowledge that we have of this word, if we know it and do not do it.

I know this is difficult to grasp since the world led us to think and believe otherwise, but the last days are upon us. Jesus Christ will be coming soon and God wants to give us a chance to make it right. Thinking about eternal life, knowing God's Word, and doing what His Word says, is imperative to having eternal life with Jesus Christ.

HOSEA 3:1-3

"The Lord said to me, "Go again, love a woman who is loved by a love and is committing adultery, just like the love of the Lord for the children of Israel, who look to other gods and love the raisin cakes of the pagans.

So I bought her for myself for fifteen shekels of silver, and one and one-half homers of barley.

And I said to her, "You shall stay with me many days; you shall not play the harlot, nor shall you have a man so, too, will I be towards you."

*H*osea had a wife named Gomer, who was a harlot, going from lover to lover. She left Hosea for harlotry. Hosea was a faithful husband.

In this book God Himself, instructs Hosea to take back Gomer, his unfaithful wife. This symbolizes God's devotion to seek reconciliation; even if it means being subjected to humiliation. Humiliation comes from the word humility, humble yourself. Not only did Hosea take his wife back, but he promised to treat her as if she never was unfaithful. Hosea did not do this on his own strength, but God gave him the strength that he needed to do what God asked him to do. This is a demonstration of God's love and ideals towards restoration and reconciliation.

HOSEA 14:1,2

*O Israel, return to the Lord your God, for you
have stumbled because of your iniquity.
Take words with you,
And return to the Lord.
Say to Him,
"Take away all iniquity;
Receive us graciously,
for we will offer the sacrifices of our lips."*

The children of Israel repented to God. This is an illustration that if we would repent to God when we sin, He will fulfill all His promises in our life. If we read on, we would see what happens after the children repented.

HOSEA 14:4-7

"I will heal their backsliding;
I will love them freely,
For my anger has turned away from him.
I will be like the dew to Israel;
He shall grow like the lily,
and lengthen his roots like Lebanon.
His branches shall spread;
His beauty shall be like an olive tree,
And his fragrance like Lebanon.
Those who dwell under his shadow shall return;
They shall be revived like grain,
and grow like a vine.
Their scent shall be like the wine of Lebanon.

*T*he Lord restored Israel and restored His blessing. Revived Israel is described as a beautiful lily. This is God's demonstration, His example, to who we should be to one another. If God can do it for us, He expects us to do it for others. One of Jesus' last commands was *John 15:17*, *"These things I command you, that you love one another."*

Life after divorce could lead to SIN, whether the husband or wife committed sexual immorality before the divorce or not. Each person that is divorced and enters into a relationship after divorce, commits adultery according to *Matthew 5:32, "Whoever marries a woman who is divorced commits adultery."* This is for men and women. The exception clause *does not* mean that once sexual immorality takes place that you must give a divorce.

If there was no sexual sin before the divorce, the husband who divorces his wife, giving her the opportunity to enter into a relationship with another man, will be accountable to God for causing his wife to commit adultery by divorcing her.

If the wife commits sexual immorality and the husband chooses to divorce her, and the wife chooses to remarry, the husband did not cause her to commit adultery, therefore he is not accountable, because she chose to sin before the divorce and after the divorce. If, after her husband divorces her, she repents to God, remains unmarried and out of sexual sin, and chooses to live righteous and holy before God, God will honor her obedience to His Word. God gave us the gift of grace and mercy.

Marriage is a gift from God, a blessing. If you receive the gift, Honor it. Every gift that God created for us is good and blessed. How could we not receive a good gift?

LUKE 16:18

"Whoever divorces his wife and marries another commits adultery; and whoever marries her who is divorced from her husband commits adultery."

*M*arriage is lifelong. Let's put away immorality and upkeep our standards of high morals for ourselves. Our body is a temple of God.

Violence and sexual immorality attacks the temple of God. Be a covenant Keeper. Let us preserve this temple for God's Work.

ROMANS 12:9-11

"Let love be without hypocrisy. Abhor what is evil. Cling to what is good.

Be kindly affectionate to one another with brotherly love, in honor giving preference to one another;

not lagging in diligence, fervent in spirit, serving the Lord."

The highest form of Love is "Agape Love" this is self-sacrificial love. This is the act whereby one person seeks the best for another, sacrificing oneself for another. This is the love God desires for husbands and wives and all of mankind. Christ is the model for such sacrificial love.

1 CORINTHIANS 7:10-14

"Now to the married I command, yet not I but the Lord: A wife is not to depart from her husband.

But even if she does depart, let her remain un-married or be reconciled to her husband. And a husband is not to divorce his wife.

But to the rest I, not the Lord says: If any brother has a wife who does not believe, and she is willing to live with him, let him not divorce her.

And a woman who has a husband, who does not believe, if he is willing to live with her, let her not di-vorce him.

For the unbelieving husband is sanctified by the wife and the unbelieving wife is sanctified by the hus-band, otherwise your children will be unclean, but now they are holy."

*F*irst Corinthians clearly states, that "A wife is not to depart or divorce her husband and if she does, she must remain unmarried or reconcile to her husband." *This does not require further explanation.* It also states, "a husband is not to divorce his wife." A husband and a wife should not leave each other; it is not God's desire for marriage. Jesus thought this in Mark 10:9-12.

"Unbelieving" means that the husband or wife does *not* believe in God at all, does not believe that there is a God; atheist or agnostic. "Unbelieving does *not* qualify when both parties believe in Jesus Christ and one goes to a church and the other is not happy with that church and there is some differences in opinions, or the other party is not ready to begin attending church on a full time or regular basis. Once the husband or wife believes Jesus Christ is the Son of God, that He was sent by God to die for our sins, was crucified on the cross, died, buried and was resurrected on the third day to save the world from sin and iniquity they can no longer be considered an unbeliever. Some men and women may be saved and have backslidden, turned away from God, but that does not make them an "unbeliever or unevenly yolked."

We are not to condemn. If a husband or wife is not saved, it is our call as the saved husband or wife to lead them to Christ, mainly by the life we live in Christ. We must be steadfast and consistent in our walk and try not to condemn the backslider or unsaved person.

1 CORINTHIANS 7:14 — "For the unbelieving husband is sanctified by the wife and the unbelieving wife is sanctified by the husband, otherwise your children will be unclean, but now they are holy."

For if we have Jesus Christ living on the inside of us, *John 8:12 — "I am the light of the world,"* then the light lives on the inside of us and if we are the light, he who is unsaved will eventually follow the light. It may take some time, but where there is light, darkness will not prevail, light always lights up a dark room.

JOHN 3:17 — *"For God did not send his Son into the world to condemn the world, but that the world through Him might be saved."*

1 CORINTHIANS 7:39,40 — *"A wife is bound by law as long as her husband lives;*

but if her husband dies, she is at liberty to be married to whom she wishes, only in the Lord."

I cannot emphasize enough that marriage is "lifelong." This is the only place in the Bible and also *Romans 7:2* that re-marriage is spoken of or permitted and that is when a marriage partner dies. There is one restriction and that is that you must marry someone that is in Christ.

EPHESIANS 5:22-33

Wives, submit to your own husbands, as to the Lord.

For the husband is head of the wife, as also Christ is the head of the church; and He is the savior of the body.

Therefore, just as the church is subject to Christ, so let the wives be to their own husbands in everything.

Husbands, love your wives, just as Christ also loved the church and gave Himself for her

that He might sanctify and cleanse her with the washing of water by the word,

that He might present her to Himself a glorious church, not having spot or wrinkle or any such thing, but that she should be holy and without blemish.

So husbands ought to love their own wives as their own bodies; he who loves his wife loves himself.

For no one ever hated his own flesh but nourishes and cherishes it, just as the Lord does the church.

For we are members of His body, of His flesh and of His bones.

"For this reason a man shall leave his father and mother and be joined to his wife, and the two shall become one flesh."

This is a great mystery, but I speak concerning Christ and the church.

Nevertheless let each one of you in particular so love his own wife as himself, and let the wife see that she respects her husband.

*J*ust as Christ is not inferior to the Father, but is the second person in the Trinity, so wives are equal to their own husbands. Yet in a marriage relationship, a husband and a wife have different roles to the LORD. A wife's voluntary submission arises out of her own submission to Christ. He calls on husbands to love self-sacrificially. Husbands are to emulate Christ's love; the kind of love that is willing to lay down one's life for another person and serve that person even if it means suffering. Jesus loved the Church so much that He was willing to suffer and die for it. His actions not only saved the Church but sanctified it. Jesus wanted to develop the Church into what it should be, the Holy Temple.

A husband who realizes that his wife is truly his own flesh will treat her with love and care and will be willing to sacrifice himself for her. The Christian marriage parallels the union that exists spiritually between *Christ* and His bride, *the Church*. Husbands, put aside your own likes, desires, opinions, preferences and welfare to please your wife and meet her needs. Then you are truly dying to self to live for your wife. This is what Christ's love demands. Love always seeks to purify. Just as the Body of Christ is indivisible, God's ideal for marriage is that it be indivisible. As Christ is one with His Church, you husbands are one with your wives.

COLOSSIANS 3:8
"But now you yourselves are to put off all these: anger, wrath, malice, blasphemy, filthy language, out of your mouth."

COLOSSIANS 3:12
"Therefore, as the elect of God, holy and beloved, put on tender mercies, kindness, humility, meekness, longsuffering."

COLOSSIANS 3:14-15
"Bearing with one another and forgiving one another if anyone has complaint against another, even as Christ forgave you, so you must do.

But above all these things put on Love which is the bond of perfection.

And let the peace of God rule in your hearts to which also you were called in one body and be thankful."

COLOSSIANS 3:18,19
"Wives, submit to your husbands, as it is fitting to the Lord. Husbands, love your wives and do not be bitter toward them."

1 THESSALONIANS 4:3-8

"For this is the will of God, your sanctification: that you should abstain from sexual immorality;

that each of you should know how to possess his own vessel in sanctification and honor,

not in passion of lust, like the Gentiles who do not know God;

that no one should take advantage of and defraud his brother in this matter, because the Lord is the avenger of all such, as we also forewarned you and testified.

For God did not call us to uncleanness, but in holiness.

Therefore he who rejects this does not reject man, but God, who has also given us His Holy Spirit."

*T*he human body is a temple; it is God's temple and should be kept holy. The body should be honored, as it is created by God, and should be sanctified in keeping with its holy purpose. Believers should have a personal passion for sexual purity that surpasses the sexual passion that the world has for sexual experiences. Sexual involvement outside of marriage dishonors God. When we reject holiness we are directly rejecting God and the Holy Sprit that lives on the inside of us.

Sex within marriage is viewed as a good gift from God to be enjoyed and celebrated by both husband and wife. *Proverbs 5:15-20; Hebrews 13:4.*

Lust is a strong desire for anything. However, in the sexual context, lusts are defined as "the sinful desire for illicit sex." Lust is forbidden by God because it gives birth to sin, which leads to death.

(Matthew 5:28; Romans 13:13; James 1:14, 15 Peter 4:3)

Adultery is extramarital sex.

PROVERB 6:32 — "*Whoever commits adultery with a woman, lacks understanding. He who does so destroys his own soul.*" It is very important to know this.

How can we stay pure in an impure world?

- By living carefully according to Gods Word and hiding it in our hearts (Psalm 119:19-11).
- By making the conscious choice not to lust (Job 31:1).
- By walking under the control of the Holy Spirit (Galatians 5:16-25).
- By fleeing sexual temptation and pursuing righteousness (2 Timothy 2:22).

TITUS 2:4,5

"That they admonish (encourage) the young women to love their husbands, to love their children, to be discreet, chaste, homemakers, good, obedient to their own husband, that the word of God may not be blasphemed."

*P*aul here speaks of love in the form of commitment of a woman to her husband's welfare. Women are required to honor their husbands, so that their actions would glorify God, build His kingdom, and strengthen the family.

My beloved brothers and sisters, "love your wives," "love your husbands." Love them with your hearts and not your needs. God gave us the gift of love. Use the gift. Ask God to fill your hearts with His love, to love your partner, in spite of the hurts, or pain they may have caused you in the marriage. "Love conquers all." *Proverbs 10:12 states, "Love covers all sins."* It is better to love than to be loved. It is better to give than to receive. Take the hurts and pains and combine it with your love for Jesus in your hearts, and I promise you, the final product will be "Godly Love." Jesus demonstrated His love for us by dying for us even though we are sinners. Is there greater love than this? We should strive to have the same kind of love and share it while we are on this earth. Love is not love until we share.

God can cause you to forget the deteriorated years from your marriage when things didn't seem good, look good, or feel good. He can cause you to see a new season for your marriage beyond your imagination. If you can see it, you can receive it. If He gives you a vision, He can bring it to pass.

HEBREWS 13:4

"Marriage is honorable among all, and the bed undefiled; but fornicators and adulterers God will judge."

The marriage bed is sacred, and God expects that we honor it and protect it.

Adulterers, adulteresses, fornicators, you will be judged. God is waiting for you to come to Him in repentance.

1 PETER 2:11,12

"Beloved, I beg you as sojourners and pilgrims, abstain from fleshly lusts which war against the souls,

having your conducts honorable among Gentiles, that when they speak against you as evildoers, they may, by your good works which they observe, glorify God in the day of visitation."

*L*et's keep in mind that the earth is not our home; we are foreigners traveling through this earth to our final destination, our eternal home, heaven. We need to stay aware and keep away from the urge to self-indulge. Life is a war to be waged, and this war leads to eternal life or death.

The life we live will either bring glory to God with our good works or bring shame and destruction on ourselves by evil works.

1 PETER 3:1

*"Wives, likewise, be submissive to your own hus-
bands, that even if some do not obey the word, they,
without the word may be won by the conduct of their
wives."*

$\mathcal{P}$eter is speaking to the wives to be submissive to your husbands so that, if anyone of them does not believe the Word, they may be won over without words, but by the behavior of their wives, when they see the purity and reverence of your lives.

Our first marriage should be to the family. If we are not meeting the needs of our family, what do you have to offer the world? Should you say to God, "Lord I am sorry, but my ministry takes priority over my marriage. I still care deeply, but I have priorities and my marriage is getting in the way?" What would God think about this?

In the Church today people are leaving off preaching the unadulterated Word of God in the name of purpose and effectiveness and numerical growth at the expense of *TRUTH, CHRISTIAN MATURITY AND DISCIPLINE.*

1 PETER 3:4
"Let it be the hidden man of the heart, in that which is not corruptible, even the ornament of a meek and quiet spirit, which is in the sight of God of Great Price."

*O*ur beauty should not come from our outward adorn-
ment, but it should be that of our inner self, the unfad-
ing beauty of a gentle and quiet spirit, which is of great
worth in God's sight. For this is the way the holy women of
the past who put their hope in God used to make themselves
beautiful. They were submissive to their husbands, like
Sarah, who obeyed Abraham and called him her master.
We are the daughters of Sarah, if we do what is right and do
not give way to fear of inferiority.

Submission to our husbands does not mean we as
women have been relegated to an inferior position of servi-
tude that denies us of being unfulfilled. Wives, submission
to our husbands is an "Act of Obedience" to God on our part,
that does not diminish our worth in anyway. A woman who
adorns herself with the imperishable quality of a "gentle
and quiet spirit" is "precious" to God.

1 PETER 3:7

Like wise, ye husbands, dwell with them according to knowledge, giving them according to knowledge, giving honor unto the wife, as unto the weaker vessel as being heirs together of the grace of life, that your prayers may not be hindered."

*P*eter is saying to the husbands in the same way, to be considerate as you live with your wives, and treat them with respect as the weaker partner and as heirs with you, of the gracious gift of life, so that nothing will hinder your prayers. Wives have power when they obey God's commands, when they do what is required. When husbands don't do what is required, their prayers are hindered. Plain and simple. We have power in obedience to the Word of God.

1 PETER 3:8,9,12,13

"Finally, be ye all of one mind, having compassion one of another, love as brethren, be pitiful, be courteous.

Not rendering evil for evil railing for railing, but contrariwise blessing knowing that you are there unto called, that ye should inherit a blessing.

For the eyes of the Lord are over the righteous and his ears are open to their prayers, but the face of the Lord is against them that do evil.

And who is he that will harm you if ye be followers of that which is good."

*P*eter is saying, who is going to harm you if you are eager to do well? But even if you should suffer for what is right, you are blessed. Do not fear what they fear; do not be frightened. Being submissive is clearly not that of a master to slave, as many of us women may think, it is that of a head to a body. God is the head of Jesus, Jesus is the head of our husband, and our husband is the head of the wife. The head gives guidance and directions to the body. I know you must be thinking that your husbands are in no way capable of guiding you or giving you directions. A woman may be thinking that she is smarter than her husband. While this may be true, she is still under the law to be submissive. She can share her feelings and input; taking note that she is not being denied her input in decisions, it is the manner in which she handles herself when giving her input, opinion, or ideas. It must be done in a graceful manner, with peace in mind and not with control.

Sometimes the husband may not handle the situation in the right way or they may be the ones trying to be dominating and controlling, but as the wiser vessel, a godly wife, an obedient wife, may have to look in the other direction and just leave it alone, letting God take control. When these situations arise, look in the opposite direction, say a silent prayer in your heart, "Lord, I put him/her in your hands. You take control of this situation." And sure enough, without a fight, or disagreement, God works it out. God will make a husband see a point that a wife cannot help him to see, and they will sometimes come back to you with the same suggestion that you had first.

When you are obedient to God and give Him control, He can fix situations that you could not fix if you spent your whole life trying to fix them. God will not respond to us as wives in our marriage if we are not obedient to the marital laws, for He does not endorse *"rebellion."* Our prayers would not be answered or we would not see God move in our lives and marriage as a direct result of our refusal to submit to our husbands. This could result in family dysfunctions. Beware; satan would try to keep wives from submitting to husbands, in order to create war and dysfunction.

God wants women who are connected to Him and know Him to be attractive in their spirits by means of good works. God wants wives who will honor Him in whatever circumstances they may fall into, and he offers wives, the "power" to pull this off in the midst of your imperfect settings. It is a challenge that comes with great rewards in marriage.

"ALL GREATNESS IS BORN OUT OF ADVERSITY"

A woman who follows after God needs to understand her great value in God's sight, even if her husband doesn't see or appreciate it. God will work on your behalf. God will work to bring your spouse in line. He will fix whatever needs to be fixed in your marriage without your help or doings.

"A wife's inner transformation by God is one of the most effective change formulas for marriages. Inner beauty gets more attractive with each passing year."

A husband may be attracted to your external beauty, but your internal beauty will change him and bring happiness, joy and perfection in your marriage. God will do what you cannot do, fix what you can never fix and touch areas you can not touch in your marriage.

Jesus trusted in God when he was suffering on the cross. He was beaten, stoned and tormented, but he did not rebel. He did not say a bad word to the men who tormented him. In the same manner, as Jesus trusted in God in His testing situation, so wives, who are responsible for the happiness, joy and success of the family and the home, you have to trust God even in a bad marriage or situation. As wives you need to bear your suffering patiently, and allow God to do his complete work in your marriage, and your husbands, as Jesus did on the Cross. God will liberate us from fear of being taken advantage of.

I urge all wives to try God's way. Mouthing off to your husbands with dishonorable words, has done nothing for you thus far. Then you need to try it God's way. When we do not obey God, and you do not submit to your husband, you place yourselves between God and your husband, therefore, God cannot work on him or your marriage.

DEUTERONOMY 24:1-4

"When a man takes a wife and marries her, and it happens that she finds no favor in his eyes because he has found some uncleanness in her, and he writes her a certificate of divorce, puts it in her hand, and sends her out of his house,

when she has departed from his house, and goes and becomes another man's wife,

if the latter husband detests her and writes her a certificate of divorce, puts it in her hand, and sends her out of his house, or if the latter husband dies who took her as his wife,

then her former husband who divorced her must not take her back to be his wife after she has been defiled; for that is an abomination before the LORD, and you shall not bring sin on the land which the LORD your God is giving you as an inheritance."

*T*he woman is defiled, and it is an abomination before the Lord because, giving your wife a divorce and causing her to marry another man *(she will only be marrying legally, not by covenant, because a woman is still under covenant with her first husband until he dies and likewise a man, the second marriage is just a legal entity)* is sending her out to commit adultery. The same is true with wives who divorce their husbands. She cannot return to her first husband because she is now an adulteress. The only solution if divorce occurs is to reconcile the marriage or remain unmarried. *First Corinthians 7:11 tells us, "But even if she does depart, let her remain unmarried or be reconciled to her husband.*

"God Hates Divorce"

MALACHI 2:14-16

Yet you say, "For what reason?"
Because the Lord has been witness
Between you and the wife of your youth,
With whom you have dealt treacherously;
Yet she is your companion
And your wife by covenant.
But did He not make them one?
Having a remnant of the Spirit?
And why one?
He seeks godly offspring.
Therefore take heed to your spirit,
And let none deal treacherously with the wife of
his youth.
"For the Lord God of Israel says
That HE hates divorce,
For it covers one's garments with violence,'
Says the Lord of host.
"Therefore take heed to your spirit,
That you do not deal treacherously."

*G*od has joined a husband and a wife as one flesh. "Remnant of the Spirit" indicates the work of God's Holy Spirit in the life of the married couple. God has joined them and by His Holy Spirit He has worked on their behalf to strengthen them. "Take heed of the Spirit" indicates that we must stay in line with the Holy Spirit concerning our marriage. The Holy Spirit will lead us and guide us according to God's purpose and design for marriage.

In *Malachi* it states that God witnessed your marriage of your youth. You are companions to each other and you are husband and wife by covenant. This is a very important statement directly from God. He is reminding you that you are under covenant when you marry your husband or wife of your youth. Youth is that period of life when you are young and you feel that you are at an age to leave your father and mother, and take care of yourselves and you decide to enter into marriage. This is your husband or wife of your youth, and this is the one you leave your father and mother to cleave to.

MATTHEW 19:5,6 — "For this reason a man shall leave his father and mother and be joined to his wife, and the two shall become one flesh'?

So then, they are no longer two but one flesh. Therefore what God has joined together, let not man separate."

This is your first marriage and this is the one God honors and holds as a covenant to Him. God is telling us to listen to the Holy Spirit and do not deal treacherously with your husband or wife of your youth for He hates divorce. For when you deal treacherously with our partners it covers your garments with violence. God does not like blood covered garments.

"Friendship"

SONGS OF SOLOMON 5:16
"This is my beloved, and this is my friend."

*L*et your own husband or wife be your best friend for a lifetime.

Friendship can be a perfect gift.

PROVERBS 2:10-13

"Wisdom will enter your heart,
Knowledge will be pleasant to your soul,
Discretion will guard you,
Understanding will watch over you.
To deliver you from the way of evil
From the man who speaks perverse things,
From those who leave the paths of uprightness."

ou will know divine truth; it protects you.

Verse 16 states, "Wisdom is able to deliver you from the strange woman or man, from adulteress, adulterer who flatters with their tongues." When you know the divine wisdom of God, the discernment of God, the understanding of God, when you know what the word teaches it will deliver you from the strange woman or man, strange in the sense that he or she does not belong to you.

You cannot break up a marriage, violate a covenant, and tear up a home without tremendous consequences. It is the wisdom of God that protects you. It's having the mind of God and the mind of Christ as you approach marriage and understanding the greatness of the gift from God. If you understand what God's will is and what God desires, then God will bless your faithfulness and he'll bless you if you stay faithful to that union. That will keep you from the flattering tongue of the adulterer and adulteress that has torn down their house to death and want to do the same to yours. Love the Truth; love the instructions of God. Love the wisdom of God.

"The Harlot"

PROVERBS 5:3-6

For the lips of an immoral woman drip honey,
And her mouth is smoother than oil;
But in the end she is bitter as wormwood,
Sharp as a two-edged sword.
Her feet go down to death,
Her steps lay hold of hell.
Lest you ponder her path of life —
Her ways are unstable;
You do not know them.

"Your Own Wife"

PROVERB 5:15-20

Drink water from your own cistern
And running water from your own well.
Should your fountains be dispersed abroad
Streams of water in the streets?
Let them be only your own,
And not for strangers with you.
Let your fountains be blessed,
And rejoice with the wife of your youth.
As a loving deer and a graceful doe,
Let her breast satisfy you at all times;
And always be enraptured with her love.
For why should you, my son, be enraptured by an
immoral woman,
And be embraced in the arms of a seductress?

"The Harlot"

PROVERBS 6:24-29

To keep you from the evil woman,
From the flattering tongue of a seductress.
Do not lust after her beauty in your heart,
Nor let her allure you with her eyelids
For by means a harlot
A man is reduced to a crust of bread;
And an adulteress will prey upon his precious life.
Can a man take fire to his bosom?
And his clothes not be burned?
Can one walk on hot coals,
And his feet not be seared?
So is he who goes in to his neighbor's wife;
Whoever touches her shall not be innocent.

Be aware of the harlot. Proverbs 6:24-29 describes how she presents herself and what to look for in her actions.

"The Crafty Harlot"
PROVERBS 7:10-27

"And there a woman met him,
with the attire of a harlot, and a crafty heart.
She was loud and rebellious,
Her feet would not stay at home.
At times she was outside, at times in the open square.
Lurking around at every corner.
So she caught him and kissed him;
With an impudent face she said to him:
"I have peace offerings with me; Today I have paid
my vows
So I came out to meet you, diligently to seek your face,
And I have found you.
I have spread my bed with tapestry,
Colored coverings of Egyptians linen.
I have perfumed my bed with myrrh, aloes, and
cinnamon.
Come, let us take our fill of love until morning;
Let us delight ourselves with love.
For my husband is not at home;
He has gone on a long journey
He has taken a bag of money with him,
And will come home on the appointed day."

With her enticing speech she caused him to yield,
With her flattering lips she seduced him.

Immediately he went after her, as an ox goes to the slaughter,
Or as a fool to the correction of the stocks,
Till an arrow struck his liver.
As a bird hastens to the snare,
He did not know it would cost his life.

Now therefore, listen to me, my children;
Pay attention to the words of my mouth;
Do not let your heart turn aside to her ways
Do not stray into her paths;
For she has cast down many wounded,
And all who were slain by her were strong men.
Her house is the way to hell
Descending to the chambers of death."

Proverbs 7:10-27 describes the subtlety of the harlot and all her attributes when she makes her appearance. This is a detailed description of what to look for when approached by women. Notice in this scripture, the harlot approaches her prey first. She plots to entrap the man, her preparations and her words of invitation are evil in the sight of God. This scripture shows us how a young fool falls into sexual immorality. The young man is oblivious to his fate and has no idea how foolish he is.

"Adultery"

PROVERBS 30:20
This is the way of an adulteress woman:
She eats and wipes her mouth,
And says, "I have done nothing wicked."

*B*eware of the Harlots and seductress. This scripture illustrates their qualities.

"*A Virtuous Woman*"
PROVERBS 31:10-31

Who can find a virtuous wife?
For her worth is far above rubies
The heart for her husband safely trusts her,
So he will have no lack of gain.
She does him good and not evil
All the days of her life.
She is like the merchant ships,
She brings her food from afar.
She also rises while it is yet night,
And provides food for her household,
And a portion for her maidservants.
She considers a field and buys it;
From her profits she plants a vineyard.
She girds herself with strength,
And strengthens her arms.
She perceives that her merchandise is good,
And her lamp does not go out by night.
She stretches out her hands to the distaff,
And her hand holds spindle.
She extends her hand to the poor
Yes, she reaches out her hands to the needy.
She is not afraid of snow for her household,
For all her household is clothed with scarlet.
She makes tapestry for herself;
Her clothing is fine linen and purple.

Her husband is known in the gates,
When he sits among the elders of the land.
She makes linen garments and sells them,
And supplies sashes and sells them,
Strength and honor are her clothing;
She shall rejoice in time to come.
She opens her mouth with wisdom,
And on her tongue is the law of kindness
She watches over the ways of the household,
And does not eat of idleness.
Her children rise up and call her blessed;
Her husband also, and he praises her:
"Many daughters have done well,
But you excel them all."
Charm is deceitful and beauty is passing,
But a woman who fears the Lord, she shall be praised.
Give her of the fruits of her hands,
And let her own works praise her in the gates.

All Women should desire to be a "Virtuous Woman."

REVELATION 2:21-23

"And I gave her time to repent of her sexual immorality and she did not repent.

"Indeed I will cast her into a sickbed, and those who commit adultery with her into great tribulation, unless they repent of their deeds.

I will kill her children with death, and all the churches shall know that I am He who searches the minds and hearts. And I will give to each one of you according to your works."

This scripture speaks for itself. We all have the opportunity to repent and turn away from a lifestyle that is unpleasing to God the Father. These are consequences to be suffered for sexual immorality.

To all the women who went through a divorce that left you broken, wounded, hurt and in tremendous pain.

To the women whose husbands passed on to be with the Lord, and you did not have enough time to experience the fullness of Marriage. God can be all that you need Him to be.

This is for you:

ISAIAH 54:4-8

"Do not fear, for you will not be ashamed;
Neither be disgraced, for you will not be put to shame;
For you will forget the shame of your youth,
And will not remember the reproach of your widowhood
anymore.
For your Maker is your husband,
The LORD of hosts is His name;
And your Redeemer is the Holy One of Israel;
He is called the God of the whole earth.
For the LORD has called you
Like a woman forsaken and grieved in spirit,
Like a youthful wife when you were refused,"
Says your God.
"For a mere moment I have forsaken you,
But with great mercies I will gather you.
With a little wrath I hid My face from you for a
moment;
But with everlasting kindness I will have mercy on
you,"
Says the LORD, your Redeemer.

ISAIAH 54:10-15

For the mountains shall depart
And the hills be removed,
But My kindness shall not depart from you,
Nor shall My covenant of peace be removed,"
Says the LORD, who has mercy on you.
"O you afflicted one,
Tossed with tempest, and not comforted,
Behold, I will lay your stones with colorful gems,
And lay your foundations with sapphires.
I will make your pinnacles of rubies,
Your gates of crystal,
And all your walls of precious stones.
All your children shall be taught by the LORD,
And great shall be the peace of your children.
In righteousness you shall be established;
You shall be far from oppression, for you shall not
fear;
And from terror, for it shall not come near you.
Indeed they shall surely assemble, but not because
of Me.
Whoever assembles against you shall fall for your
sake.

*W*hen a precious relationship such as marriage comes to a sudden end through divorce or death, this is a time of grief, hurt, suffering, and feelings of rejection. But Jesus is a healer and a restorer. Divorce is the death of a marriage; this can bring feelings of rejection, lower self worth, loneliness, and brokenness.

JESUS! Jesus can bring strength, hope, comfort and encouragement through His power; power in prayer and reading the Word of God. At times like these we should become totally dependant on God.

Even though you may feel unloved and unwanted, God knows your name and He is speaking to you in Isaiah 54:4-15. God is saying in verse 4, *"Do not fear, for he will allow no shame to come upon you."*

This verse 5 and 6 really touched my heart; God is saying to women whose hearts and spirits are grieved, that "He is your Husband, when you are forsaken and refused by your earthly husband. Wives, when your husband has walked out on you, when your husband has rejected you, when your husband has caused you pain and hurt, "God, your Maker in heaven is your husband." This is a mighty expression of how much God loves all of His earthly children.

PSALMS 27:10 — "When my father and mother forsake me, then the Lord will take care of me."

The Lord can be a father and a mother to us when our parents forsake us; He can be a husband to us when we are refused and rejected; He can be a shield for me, the one who lifts up my head *(Psalms 3:3)*; a refuge *(Psalms 9:9)*; My shepherd *(Psalms 23:1)*; My light and salvation *(Psalms 27:1)*; My Helper *(Psalms 30:10)*; My rock of refuge *(Psalms 31:2)*; a father of the fatherless, a defender of widows *(Psalms 68:5)*.

My high tower, *(Psalms 144:2)*. Turn your eyes on Jesus. He will take your hand and lead you to the "rock of refuge" *(Psalms 31:2)*; to the fountain of living water *(Jeremiah 2:13)*.

ECCLESIASTES 2:26
"For God gives wisdom and knowledge and joy to a man who is good in His sight;"

*W*e all want to be blessed with wisdom and knowledge by God, and to receive this we must be obedient to His Word and so become good in His sight.

Four Promises of Forgiveness

When there is adultery, infidelity, extra-marital sex, betrayal, shame and embarrassments in a marriage, there is need for forgiveness. Through forgiveness God tears down the walls that our sins have built, and he opens the way for a renewed relationship with Him. This is exactly what we must do if we are to forgive as the Lord forgives us. We must release the person that has wronged us from the penalty of being separated from us. We must not hold wrongs against others, nor think about the wrongs, and not punish others for them. Therefore, forgiveness may be described as a decision to make four promises:

1. "I will not dwell on this incident."
2. "I will not bring up this incident again and use it against you."
3. "I will not talk to others about this incident."
4. "I will not let this incident stand between us or hinder our personal relationship."

This is what God does for us and we should do the same for our husbands or wives. No more empty promises.

The spirit filled husband loves his wife not for what she can do for him, but because of what he can do for her. This is how Christ's love works. He loves us not because there's something in us that attracts Him, not because He gains any benefit from loving us, but simply because He determines to love us and delights to bestow on us His favor.

COLOSSIANS 3:13 ——"*Bearing with one another and forgiving one another if anyone has a complaint against another, even as Christ forgave you, so you also must do. But above all these things put on love which is the bond of perfection. And let the peace of God rule in your hearts to which also you were called in one body and be thankful."*

EPHESIANS 4:26,27 — "Be angry and do not sin" Do not let the sun go down on your wrath, nor give place to the devil."

PHILIPPIANS 3:13,14 — "...Forgetting those things which are behind and reaching forward to those things which are ahead,

I press toward the goal for the prize of the upward call of God in Christ Jesus."

EPHESIANS 4:29-32

"*Let no corrupt word proceed out of your mouth, but what is good for necessary edification, that it may impart grace to the hearers.*

And do not grieve the Holy Spirit of God, by whom you were sealed for the day of redemption.

Let all bitterness, wrath, anger, clamor, and evil speaking be put away from you, with all malice.

And be kind to one another, tenderhearted, forgiving one another, even as God in Christ forgave you.

*A*s the book of Ephesians said, we grieve the Holy Spirit when we carry around anger, bitterness, and wrath and speak evil of people. Instead we must carry kindness, tenderheartedness and forgiveness in our hearts. Even to the person who has been mean and cruel to us.

God is an awesome God; he deserves more praise than our lips can ever utter to Him in our lifetime on this earth. I can only do this through Christ who strengthened me. I will do this with God's help and strength. Forgive. If we don't do this, God cannot complete his work in us and our marriage as he promised. This is a key point in this journey with God.

My brothers and sisters, marriage is not always perfect. After that beautiful day of walking down the isle, the flowers and the celebration, then comes the serious part of marriage when all the guests go home and it is just you and your new wife or new husband. Then you discover all the things about the other person you did not have the chance to discover before the marriage.

Along the way there will be differences in opinions, there will be problems, there will be trials that would require prayer, patience, commitment, and long-suffering; you may be required to look the other way when situations and circumstances arise. There may be adultery, fornication, physical and mental abuse; neglect, lack of responsibility and the list could go on.

But, I greatly emphasize to you my brothers and sisters, God does not desire any of the above listed for His children, whether you are a believer or unbeliever, we are all God's children, and he has written and planned a perfect life for us all. God values each and every one of us on this earth so much. God made us in His image and likeness.

God said in *Genesis 1:26, "Let Us make man in Our image, according to Our Likeness."* We are made to reflect His majesty on earth. And so, If you are faced with any of these situations and circumstances, God can fix All things. Any problem that may arise in our marriages, God is able and will fix, restore and deliver us from any situation that may occur in our marriages. Give it to God in prayer and supplication. God created and formed us with His own hands. He knew what we would look like before we were even conceived in our mother's womb. If He made us, He is able to repair and restore any problem that may arise in our lives to His original plan for our lives. God keeps his promises no matter how difficult the circumstances may seem.

LUKE 1:37 — "For with God, nothing will be impossible."

EPHESIANS 3:2 — "Now to Him who is able to do exceedingly abundantly above all that we ask or think, according to the power that works in us."

God is waiting for us to come to Him. Jesus Christ can save and deliver the adulterer, adulteress, the alcoholic, the drug addict, the sex addict, the abusive husband or wife, the husband or wife who ran off with the harlot. Jesus can bring him back to his family, save them and deliver them. He/She must be willing. There must be a willing party.

It is highly recommended that all marriages that are experiencing problems, seek Godly council.

PROVERBS 11:14 — "Where there is no counsel, the people fall; but in the multitude of counselors there is safety."

I say Godly council because, there are a multitude of "false prophets" in the midst of the Church body. Do not go to a pastor who had an affair with a young member of the church, divorced his wife, married the individual, and opened another church and called himself a "Pastor". Counsel from a person such as this can only tell you what he knows which is to leave your husband or wife and do what the rest of the world is doing. The blind cannot lead the blind. They will both fall into a ditch. He cannot tell you what is the sanctuary of marriage or that God sees marriage as a church, because he himself violated that law. Choose your spiritual leaders who teach no other doctrine but the doctrine of Jesus Christ. When you sit under a leader that is living in sin, you can only inherit what spirits that he/she is operating under, and this will lead to a life of sin. You would be liable to make the same mistake in sin as the person you are sitting under. It is important to have a spirit of discernment to discern what type of environment you find yourself in when looking for a place of worship. Ensure that it is a place of worship that worships God the Father, His Son and the Holy Spirit and no other. Be sure the presence of Jesus Christ and the Holy Spirit is in your place of worship.

JEREMIAH 23:1,2 — "Woe to the shepherds who destroy and scatter the sheep of my pasture!" says the Lord."

...Behold I will attend to you for the evil of your doings," says the Lord.

"Love"

1 CORINTHIANS 13:4-8

Love suffers long and is kind;

Love does not envy;

Love does not parade itself, is not puffed up;

Love does not behave rudely, does not seek its own, is not provoked, thinks no evil;

Does not rejoice in iniquity, but rejoices in the truth.

Love bears all things, believes all things, hopes all things, endures all things.

Love never fails."

ove is determining what is best for another person and then doing it.

This is the God kind of Love — Agapé Love.

Love is never giving up, knowing that God can change lives for the better.

Love is an act of the will

It is a voluntary devotion.

It involves sacrifice, consideration, chivalry, communion, courtesy,

And commitment.

If we are willing to obey God, by the power of God's Spirit, we can muster that kind of love for our husband or wife...

My saints, our marriage is a testimony to the relationship between Christ and His bride, the Church. Your marriage will either tell the truth about that relationship, or it will tell a lie. What is your marriage saying to the watching world?

If you'll walk in the power of the Spirit, yield to His Word, and be mutually submissive, you can know that God will bless you abundantly and glorify His Son through your marriage.

"LOVE IS NOT LOVE UNTIL YOU SHARE IT."

My dearest brothers who are husbands and my dearest sisters who are wives, keep your eyes on the wife or husband that God has joined you with from your youth *(Malachi 2:14)*.

Take no thought to go outside of your marriage to find pleasure and fulfill fantasies, looking for things to satisfy your vain imaginations, that you may think your wife or husband may not possess. God has given you everything you need and want in a wife or husband. Anything that you think is lacking, God could fulfill and fix everything that needs fixing in your marriage."

JAMES 4:2 "You have not, because you ask not."

I often times hear men and women complain that their wife or husband is not doing things the way they want, then they proceed to go outside of their marriage to find what they think might satisfy their fantasies. Be aware of the devices of satan. *Psalm 139:8, "The Lord will perfect that which concerns me."* This tells me that everything that God gives me He will perfect it if it is imperfect; God can make it perfect.

"THERE IS BEAUTY IN EVERY IMPERFECTION." THERE IS STRENGTH IN EVERY WEAKNESS."

For the men who are abusive to their wives, this is a sign of fear, and this is what the Bible says about fear: 1 John 4:18, *"There is no fear in love, but perfect love casting out fear, because fear hath torment. He that feareth is not perfect in Love."*

I want to share with you a word that God spoke to me personally. The word is:

"For the things you see in the natural, it is temporary, subject to change; The things that are unseen are permanent."

If you are praying and trusting God for a better marriage, restoration or reconciliation, have faith in God, do not focus on what the situation looks like in front of you, because it is temporary. Focus on what God places in your heart. *If God allows you to see a better marriage, if He gave you the desire to have a better marriage, He will bring it to pass, because He first gave you the desire.*

Husbands, cover your wife in prayer. Wives, cover your husband in prayer at all times. Prayer answers all things. Husbands you are the priest of your home. Cover and protect your home and family in prayer.

I would like to share a testimony with you that blessed me and would demonstrate what the mighty power of God could do in your marriage, if you put faith and trust in Him. A testimony is like a thousand sermons.

One afternoon I came home from work, and I turned on the television to a gospel channel that I frequently watched. There was a woman sharing her testimony about her mar-

riage and what God did for her marriage. And her testimony goes like this: She and her husband were married for eleven years and had two kids. After eleven years, the husband left her with the two kids; divorced her. She lost her house and all that she had. The kids were little and she didn't have a job. She lived by faith.

It was many years of trials and tribulation, since all of this was sudden. She lived on prayer, reading her Bible and believing that God would restore her marriage. She believed God, trusted God, and had great faith everyday for seventeen years. She never looked at another man, never dated another man during the seventeen years. She kept her eyes on "the creator of the earth; the Mighty One who created the rivers to flow and the wind to blow; the One who spoke and said "let there be light," and there was light. God the Father. The One that loves us when no one else loves us. The One who said, **"I will never leave you nor forsake you," Hebrews 13:5**.

One day, after seventeen years, her husband came back home. She never gave up; she trusted God. She stood on his word and she believed.

If God could do it for her, He can do it for you. He can restore and reconcile your marriage, if you dare to trust Him, seek Him, have faith in Him, and believe every word that proceeds out of His mouth.

CONCLUSION

*I*f you have read this book and you feel in your heart that you have not been in right standing with God in any area of your marriage, if you feel your need to examine your heart and make some things right before the Lord; maybe you have done things that you are not aware is unpleasing to God; maybe it was deliberate sin, meaning that you knew it was wrong, but temptation got the better of you; maybe you are in a marriage where there is great pain and hurt, and this has caused you to slip away from God; maybe the hurt has led you down the wrong path in life; maybe you have taken your neighbor's wife, your sister's husband, your friend's husband, or wife. Maybe you have entered into adultery; fornication; abuse; mistreating your partner; making yourself superior to your partner; maybe you have left your wife or husband for another. Whatever it is, it is not too late.

GOD LOVES YOU! I do not want to end this book without inviting you to come to Jesus; His arms are open and waiting for you to come into his arms right now.

You know when Daddy or Mommy opens the door and their children run into the outstretched arms of their parents, there is great expectation of warmth, love and security in those waiting arms. Our Father in heaven is waiting, arms open wide, for us to run to Him; *GOD LOVES YOU*, and He wants you in His kingdom. Surrender to God, arms outstretched, give your heart to Jesus. All that He requires of you is just to *repent*, tell Him that you are sorry for all the wrongs you have done, all the pain or hurt you have caused your husband or wife. Turn to Jesus: Jesus suffered and died for our sins. Our sins have already been redeemed when Jesus gave His last breath on the cross. Believe in Jesus and you shall have remissions of sin. It is a decision you have to make to turn to God with faith that He could save you from a life of sin and give you everlasting life.

JOHN 3:15-17 — "That whoever believes in Him should not perish but have everlasting life.

For God so loved the world that He gave His only begotten Son, that whoever believes in Him should not perish, but have everlasting life.

For God did not send His Son into the world to condemn the world, but that the world through Him might be saved."

We don't have to live with sin; Jesus hung on the cross for every sin that you entered into. Place your sin where it belongs, on the cross. Repent to God for every wrong that you feel in your heart that you have done. This is between you and God, no one else has to know. Tell it all to God, He wants to hear you say it. When you confess it to Him; He will cast it into the Sea of forgetfulness. We must trust Jesus Christ to forgive our sins and determine to obey Him for the rest of our lives. That way we can know God and find peace again.

PSALMS 24:3 — "Who may stand in His Holy place? He who has clean hands and a pure heart."

MICAH 7:19 — "He will again have compassion on us, and subdue our iniquities. You will cast all our sins into the depths of the sea."

"God may not take you where you want to go, but He will take you where you need to be."

LIFE BEGINS AND ENDS WITH YOU. CHOOSE JESUS!

If you know in your heart that you are not right with God and you want to make it right with the Lord; if you have read this book and you want to give your life to Jesus Christ as your Lord and Savior and you feel a drawing inside to be closer to Jesus, then join me in the prayer below.

JOHN 6:44 — "No one can come to me unless the Father who sent me draws him."

Romans 10:9,10 — "that if you confess with your mouth the Lord Jesus and believe in your heart that God has raised Him from the dead, you will be saved.

For with the heart one believes unto righteousness, and with the mouth confession is made unto salvation.

Join Me In Prayer

Jesus, I love you, I repent of all of my sins.

I thank you for dying on the cross for me. I believe that you died, shed your blood to save me. I celebrate Your resurrection this beautiful day by giving my life to You; I invite You into my heart, into my life, into my home. Come Lord Jesus, I accept You as my Lord and Savior.

Come now and fill me with Your Spirit. Fill me Lord Jesus with Your love and send me forth to my family and friends to share with them Your love and Your concern. Jesus, I love You and I shall follow You all the days of my life.

Sign your name.

Date

You have just made the most important decision in your life, to accept Jesus into your life. May God bless you today and everyday for the rest of your life! May you continue in Christ and stay in Christ; learning more about Him; knowing more about Him and seeking to build a closer relationship and become more connected to Him.

God loves you. And He wants you in His kingdom. He wants to be in your life. Simple equation: Give your life to God — God will give you eternal life.

"Do not aim for a perfect life; aim for a perfect heart."

As you draw closer to God, He will teach you His ways and give you His strength. It is important to spend time in prayer everyday. Your spirit must be fed in order for growth to occur in your walk with the Lord. We have access to His presence anytime. We need to pray by simply talking to our Heavenly Father.

1JOHN 5:13 — *"These things I have written to you who believe in the name of the Son of God, that you may know you have eternal life and that you may continue to believe in the name of the Son of God."*

THIS IS MY PRAYER FOR EVERYONE READING THIS BOOK

Heavenly Father,

I bless You, I Honor You, I Praise You, and I magnify You this day.

I come boldly before Your throne today, I lift my brother/sister before You today, and I ask You father to look upon their hearts, Lord. We have all sinned and fall short of Your glory, but because of Your grace and mercy, because of Your love for us, You sent Your only begotten Son, to die for us, that our sins would be forgiven. He was wounded for our transgression and bruised for our iniquities.

I take authority over satan and every principality, every demonic spirit and all spiritual wickedness in high places, and I bind them from all marriages on this earth. I cast down every spirit of arguing, fussing, fighting and division, by the authority of Jesus Christ. Lord, give them back their marriages and the years that have deteriorated; give them back the Love that has been stolen by the enemy; let their marriage live and not die and declare the works of the Lord; that they will not walk in a diminished level, but in the Spirit. Father, if they have felt like they have missed the season for their marriage, and the enemy is telling them that they cannot get it back, Give them another season.

JOEL 2:25 — "So I will restore to you the years that the swarming locust has eaten, the crawling locust, the consuming locust, and the chewing locust."

Lord, I ask you to wash my brother/sister from his/her sins, cleanse him/her, purge them with hyssop (Psalm 51:7). Cleanse him/her with the blood of Jesus Christ because only the blood can make him/her whole again. Search their hearts and minds and remove any thoughts, feelings, desires, wants, needs that are not pleasing to you.

Lord, let there be a peace within, a peace that surpasses all understanding, joy unspeakable; a joy to serve you Lord (Psalm 139). Lord, heal their broken hearts, their hurts and pains, for you said in Psalms 147:3, "You heal the brokenhearted and bind up their wounds."

I speak freedom from bondages in marriages, for "who the Son sets free, is free indeed." (John: 36). Lord, I decree and declare peace, harmony, love, affection, unity and everything that you, Father God have promised for marriages. Renew their minds and their hearts so that they can see each other attractive, exciting and become more sensitive to each other's needs.

I ask this in the name of Jesus Christ. Amen. Praise God! All glory and honor to our Father in Heaven.

*"God Bless You
and
Your Marriage
This Day."*

If you need prayer,
You can call this prayer line that is open
24 hrs /7days per week.
New Greater Bethel Ministries
215-32 Jamaica Ave
Queens Village, NY, 11428
718-978-HELP